Someone's singing, Lora

Hymns and songs for children
chosen by Beatrice Harrop

with PIANO accompaniments,
with chords for GUITAR, and with parts
for descant recorders, glockenspiel, chime bars
and percussion

A & C Black · London

Published by A & C Black (Publishers) Ltd, 35 Bedford Row, London WC1R 4JH, © 1973, A & C Black Ltd
Reprinted 1973, 1974, 1976, 1978, 1979, 1982 (with guitar chord diagrams), 1984 (with new illustrations), 1987
Photocopying prohibited. All rights reserved. No part of this publication may be reproduced, stored in a retrieval system, or transmitted in any form or by any means without the prior permission of A & C Black Ltd
Illustrations copyright 1984
ISBN 0-7136-1730-6

Printed in Great Britain by Hollen Street Press Limited, Slough, Berkshire

---

Contents

Guitar chords

Welcome the day

1 Father, we thank you for the night
2 The golden cockerel
3 Morning has broken

Shout for joy

4 O Lord! Shout for joy!
5 Lord, I love to stamp and shout
6 I have seen the golden sunshine
7 Come, let us remember the joys of the town

This is a lovely world

8 This is a lovely world
9 To God who makes all lovely things
10 Over the earth is a mat of green
11 The sun that shines across the sea
12 I love the sun
13 We praise you for the sun

Giving thanks

14 Stand up, clap hands, shout thank you, Lord
15 Think of a world without any flowers
16 For all the strength we have

No litter, no junk

17 Milk bottle tops and paper bags

Eyes, ears, hands and feet

18 Give to us eyes
19 He gave me eyes so I could see
20 Praise to God for things we see
21 Hands to work and feet to run

Our friend and father

22 I'm very glad of God
23 Kum ba yah
24 A little tiny bird
25 Can you count the stars?
26 When lamps are lighted
27 God bless the grass that grows through the crack

Following our leader

28 The journey of life
29 I danced in the morning
30 Now Jesus one day
31 It fell upon a summer day
32 Who's that sitting in the sycamore tree?
33 Jesus' hands were kind hands
34 When a knight won his spurs

Being a friend

35 When I needed a neighbour
36 Look out for loneliness
37 If I had a hammer
38 Think, think on these things
39 The ink is black, the page is white
40 O Jesus, we are well and strong

Caring for animals

41 All things which live below the sky
42 I love God's tiny creatures
43 Little birds in winter time
44 Who built the ark?

Stars and space

45 5, 4, 3, 2, 1 and zero
46 Twinkle, twinkle, little star
47 God who put the stars in space

The year round

48 All the flowers are waking (SPRING)
49 In the early morning (SPRING)
50 Hurray for Jesus (PALM TIDE)
51 We have a king who rides a donkey (EASTER)
52 Who can see the great wind blow? (WHITSUNTIDE)
53 The flowers that grow in the garden (SUMMER)
54 Look for signs that summer's done (AUTUMN)
55 When the corn is planted (HARVEST)
56 The farmer comes to scatter the seed (HARVEST)
57 See how the snowflakes are falling (WINTER)

Going home

58 At half past three we go home to tea
59 We're going home

Index of first lines

Guitar chords

The following are the guitar chords found in this book. In some of the songs, unusual chords have been indicated. If you can play them they will add colour and interest to your accompaniments. However, you may find it easier when these occur to substitute a common chord of the same letter name (major or minor as required). For example, the chord of A may be played where A13 is marked; Em may be played for Em9; G may be played instead of Gsus4, etc.

A cross above a string means that it should not be sounded. A bracket linking two or more strings indicates that they should be held down simultaneously by the first finger. Optional or added notes (as in C add 4) are indicated by broken circles.

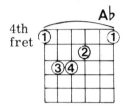

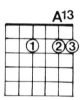
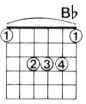
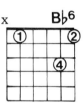
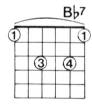

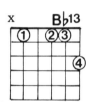

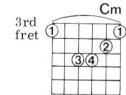

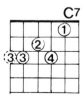
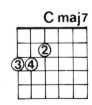
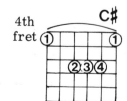

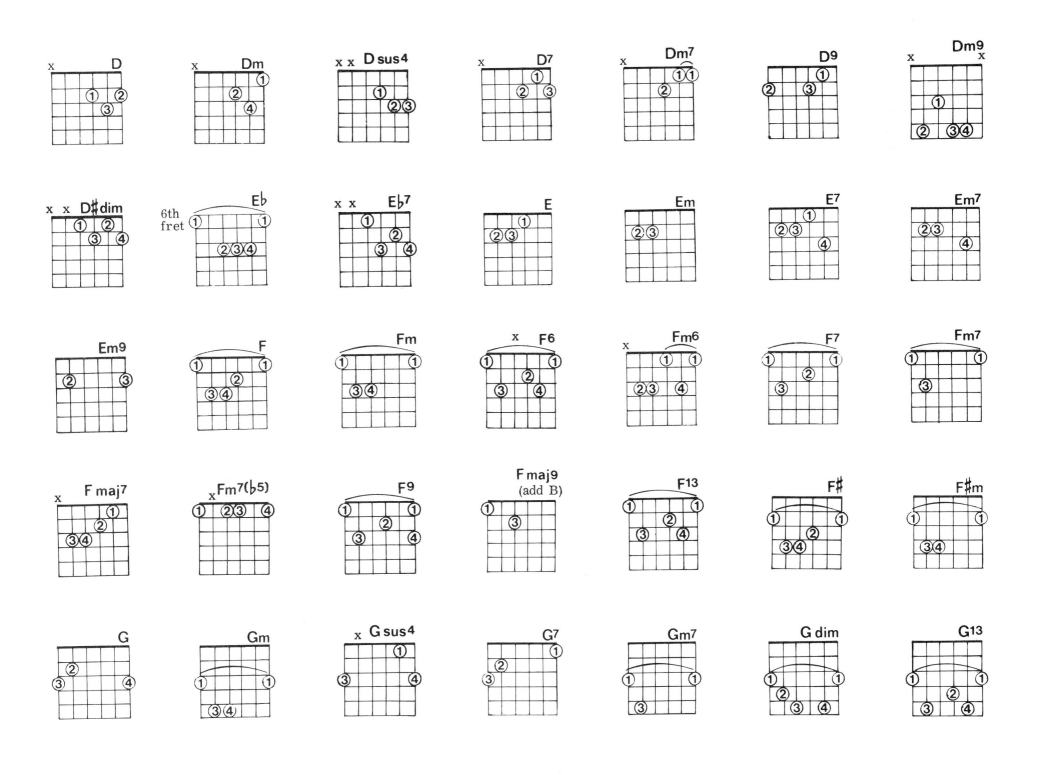

Acknowledgements

For help in compiling this selection of hymns, the publishers are grateful to Pat Lloyd, Deputy Head of Great Staughton County Primary School, Huntingdon, and to Peggy Blakeley. They also thank Mary Collins, Head of Grange County Infant School, Gosport, Hampshire, Sarah Evans of Newton Hall Nursery, Durham City, and Ian Wragg, R.E. Adviser to Derbyshire Education Committee, for helpful advice and suggestions.

Hymns 17, 18, 36, 38, 45, 54 and 59 were specially written for this book by Peggy Blakeley and Don Harper. Graham C. Westcott wrote the music to hymns 1, 15, 21, 46 (1st), 47 and the accompaniments to hymns 4, 32, 37, 44 and 51 (2nd), Roger H. Pope the music to hymn 42, and Sarah Evans the accompaniment to hymn 16 (1st), all of which are published here for the first time. Graham Westcott supplied guitar chords and Sarah Evans wrote additional instrumental parts. The music to hymn 57 and the piano accompaniments to hymns 3 (1st), 7 (1st), 9, 16, 26, 27, 40, 41, 43, 46 (2nd) and 55 (2nd) are by the music editor, Beatrice Harrop.

The following copyright owners have kindly granted their permission for the reprinting of words and music:

Sister Oswin and Geoffrey Chapman Publishers for the words and music of 32 – "Who's that sitting in the sycamore tree?" from *Let God's Children Sing*, and 30 – "Now Jesus one day" and 50 – "Hurray for Jesus" from *Sing Children of the Day*.

Crown Publishers Inc. for the words and melody of 4 – "O Lord! Shout for joy!" from *American Negro Songs and Spirituals*, edited by John W. Work, © 1940 by John W. Work.

Durham Music Ltd. for the words and music of 39 – "The ink is black, the page is white" © 1956, 1970 and 1971 by Templeton Publishing Co. Inc.

Essex Music Ltd. for the words and music of 27 – "God bless the grass" © 1964 by Schroder Music Co. and 37 – "If I had a hammer" © 1958 and 1959 by Ludlow Music Inc.

Kenneth G. Finlay for the tune of "Praise to God" (20).

Galliard Ltd for the words and music of 5 – "Lord, I love to stamp and shout" and 15 – "Think of a world without any flowers" from *New Songs for the Church*; 51 – "We have a king who rides a donkey" from *Pilgrim Praise*; and 29 – "Lord of the Dance" and 35 – "When I needed a neighbour" by Sydney Carter.

Miss D. M. Gill for the words of 7 – "Come, let us remember the joys of the town".

Dr. E. R. Goodliffe for the tune Worship (55) by the late Dr. A. H. Mann.

Granada Publishing Ltd. for the words and music of 2 – "The golden cockerel" and 58 – "At half past three" from *Morning Cockerel* by Margaret Rose and M. R. Cook, published by Rupert Hart-Davis Educational Publications Ltd.

David Higham Associates Ltd. for the words of 3 – "Morning has broken" by Eleanor Farjeon.

High-Fye Music Ltd. for the words and music of 6 – "I have seen the golden sunshine" (Friend of Jesus), 14 – "Stand up, clap hands", 28 – "The journey of life" (Follow My Leader) and 19 – "He gave me eyes" (He Made Me).

The Proprietors of *Hymns Ancient and Modern* for the second arrangement of the tune Bunessan (3).

National Christian Education Council for the words of 21 – "Hands to work and feet to run", 40 – "O Jesus, we are well and strong", 57 – "See how the snowflakes are falling", and the words and music of 43 – "Little birds in winter time".

The National Society for the words and music of 52 – "Who can see the great wind blow?", 33 – "Jesus' hands were kind hands" and 56 – "The farmer comes to scatter the seed" from *Hymns and Songs for Children*.

Oxford University Press for the words of 9 – "To God who makes all lovely things" and 49 – "In the early morning"; the tune Scots Tune (10) from *Children Praising*; the words of 34 – "When a knight won his spurs" to the tune Stowey and the tune Trefaenan (25) from *Enlarged Songs of Praise*; the melody of the tune Rodmell (41) from *The English Hymnal*; the tune Gamble (49) and the words of 42 – "I love God's tiny creatures" from *Songs of Praise for Boys and Girls*; and the tune Childhood (31) from *A Students' Hymnal*.

Miss A. M. Pullen for the words of 13 – "We praise you for the sun" and the words and music of 22 – "I'm very glad of God".

The Religious Education Press, a member of the Pergamon Group of Companies for the words and music of 12 – "I love the sun" and 48 – "All the flowers are waking" from *The Nursery Song and Picture Book* and the music arrangement of 23 – "Kum ba yah" by Colin Hodgetts from *Sing True*.

The Seabury Press for the words of 47 – "God who put the stars in space" from *Sing for Joy* © 1961 by The Seabury Press Inc. Compiled and edited by Norman and Margaret Mealy.

Laurence Swinyard for the melody of the tune Stowey (34).

The Viking Press Inc. for the words and music of 44 – "Who built the ark?" from *Rolling Along in Song* by J. Rosamond Johnson © 1937 by The Viking Press Inc.; © renewed 1965 by Mrs. Nora E. Johnson.

Josef Weinberger Ltd for the words and music of 8 – "This is a lovely world".

Every effort has been made to trace and acknowledge copyright owners. If any rights have been omitted, the Publishers offer their apologies and will rectify this in subsequent editions following notification.

The cover design and drawings are by C. R. Evans.

NB. The guitar chords have been chosen to suit the melody when accompanied by guitar alone. They do not necessarily correspond with the harmony of the piano accompaniment.

1 Father, we thank you for the night

1. Father, we thank you for the night,
   And for the pleasant morning light;
   For rest and food and loving care
   And all that makes the day so fair.

2. Help us to do the things we should,
   To be to others kind and good;
   In all we do at work or play
   To grow more loving every day.

Words: Rebecca J. Weston
Music: G. C. Westcott
Name of tune: Margaret L

2 The golden cockerel

The golden cockerel
Crows in the morning,
Wake up, children,
Welcome the day.
God's bright sun is
Riding the heavens,
Chasing sleepiness away.
Father,
Gladly we greet you,
Here come
Running to meet you.
Please be
In us and near us,
Hallowing our work and play.

Words: Margaret Rose
Music: from an old English melody

Fa—ther, Glad-ly we greet you,

Here come Run-ning to meet you. Please be

In us and near us, Hal-low-ing our work and play.

This tune will very happily take an OSTINATO and offers an excellent opportunity for this musical term to be introduced to the children.

The simple recurring theme can be played on glockenspiel, chime bars, recorder, or any other pitched instrument available.

The ostinato is printed below. Every bar is the same except the last.

LAST BAR

3 Morning has broken

1. Morning has broken
   Like the first morning,
   Blackbird has spoken
   Like the first bird.
   Praise for the singing!
   Praise for the morning!
   Praise for them, springing
   Fresh from the Lord!

2. Mine is the sunlight!
   Mine is the morning
   Here in the bright light
   Of this fair day!
   Praise with elation,
   Praise every morning
   God's re-creation
   Of the new day!

Words: Eleanor Farjeon
Name of tune: Bunessan (old Gaelic melody)

Alternative arrangement

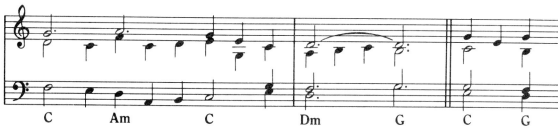
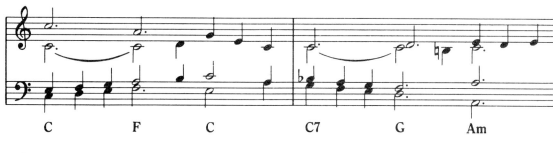
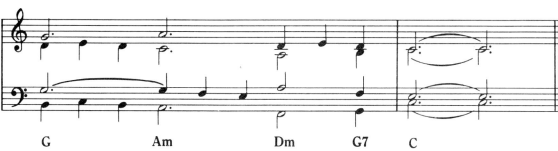

The descant recorder or glockenspiel part fits in with the simpler accompaniment on the opposite page. A second descant recorder or group of recorders could play the melody if desired.

Two piano and guitar arrangements of this tune are given so that accompanists can choose which they prefer, or play a different accompaniment to each verse.

4 O Lord! Shout for joy!

O Lord! Shout for joy!
O Lord! Shout for joy!

1. Early in the morning,
   Shout for joy!
   Early in the morning,
   Shout for joy!

2. Feel like shouting,
   Shout for joy!
   Feel like shouting,
   Shout for joy!

3. Feel like praying,
   Shout for joy!
   Feel like praying,
   Shout for joy!

4. Now I'm getting happy,
   Shout for joy!
   Now I'm getting happy,
   Shout for joy!

One suggestion for percussion accompaniment is given. Many other combinations of percussion are possible and these could be suggested by the children and reviewed by them.

Words and music: Negro spiritual
Piano accompaniment: G. C. Westcott

5 Lord, I love to stamp and shout

1. Lord, I love to stamp and shout
testing lungs and muscles out;
other times I curl up still
dreaming till I've had my fill.

2. Lord, I love to watch things fly,
whizzing, zooming, flashing by;
engines, aircraft, speedboats, cars,
spacecraft shooting to the stars.

3. Lord, I love to probe and pry
seeking out the reason why;
looking inside things and out,
finding what they're all about.

4. Lord, I'm many things and one
though my life's not long begun;
you alone my secret see
what I am cut out to be.

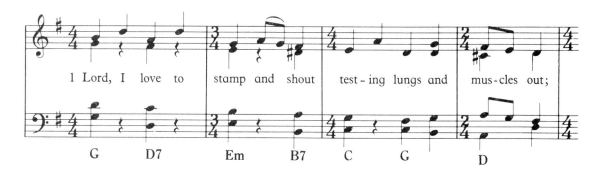

Words: Reginald Barrett-Ayres
Music: Ian Fraser

6 I have seen the golden sunshine

1. I have seen the golden sunshine,
   I have watched the flowers grow,
   I have listened to the song birds
   And there's one thing now I know,
   They were all put there for us to share
   By someone so divine,
   And if you're a friend of Jesus,
       CLAP CLAP CLAP CLAP
   You're a friend of mine.

       I've seen the light, I've seen the light,
       And that's why my heart sings.
       I've known the joy, I've known the joy
       That loving Jesus brings.

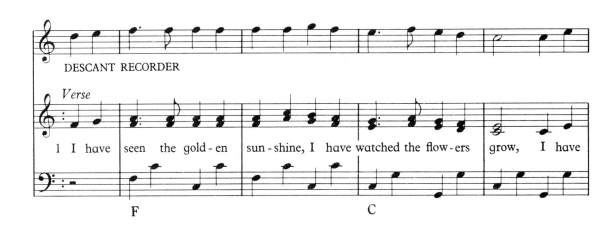

2. I have seen the morning sunshine,
   I have heard the oceans roar,
   I have seen the flowers of springtime,
   And there's one thing I am sure,
   They were all put there for us to share
   By someone so divine,
   And if you're a friend of Jesus,
       CLAP CLAP CLAP CLAP
   You're a friend of mine.

Words and music: Charlie Chester and Benny Litchfield
Title: Friend of Jesus, friend of mine

A descant recorder part is suggested to accompany the verse. As this is quite demanding on the players, no recorder part is given to accompany the chorus and players might simply listen, or join in the singing if they have sufficient breath.

As an alternative to using recorders, the children might clap or use percussion instruments to accompany the singing in the chorus, perhaps clapping on the first and third beats of each bar with an extra clap on the second beat of the fourth bar (as indicated by the crosses over the music).

7 Come, let us remember the joys of the town

1. Come, let us remember
   the joys of the town:
   Gay vans and bright buses
   that roar up and down,
   Shop windows and playgrounds
   and swings in the park,
   And street lamps that twinkle
   in rows after dark.

2. And let us remember
   the life in the street:
   The horses that pass us,
   the dogs that we meet;
   Grey pigeons, brown sparrows,
   and gulls from the sea,
   And folk who are friendly
   to you and to me.

3. We thank you, O God,
   for the numberless things
   And friends and adventures
   which every day brings.
   O may we not rest until
   all that we see
   In towns and in cities
   is pleasing to you.

Words: Doris M. Gill
Music: Welsh hymn melody
Name of tune: St Denio

Percussion might be used with this tune. Triangles and drums would make a good combination, the drums following exactly the rhythm of the notes in the bass clef and the triangles playing the following rhythm throughout:

Music : Thuringian folk song

8 This is a lovely world

1. This is a lovely world.
   Birds in the trees above
   Sing of a world that's made
   By a God of love.

2. This is a joyful world
   Where every girl and boy
   Sings of a world that's made
   By a God of joy.

To help in maintaining the rhythm and sustaining the long notes at the ends of the lines, it is suggested that children might tap out the rhythm given below on tambourine, triangle or maracas, keeping up a steady rhythm throughout the hymn.

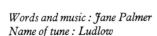

Words and music: Jane Palmer
Name of tune: Ludlow

9 To God who makes all lovely things

1. To God who makes all lovely things
   How happy must our praises be!
   Each day a new surprise he brings
   To make us glad his world to see.

2. How plentiful must be the mines
   From which he gives his gold away;
   In March he gives us celandines,
   He gives us buttercups in May.

3. On winter nights his quiet flakes
   Come falling, falling all the night,
   And when the world next morning wakes
   It finds itself all shining white.

4. He makes the sea that shines afar
   With waves that dance unceasingly;
   And every single little star
   That twinkles in the evening sky.

5. He made the people that I meet,
   The many people, great and small,
   In home and school, and down the street,
   And he made me to love them all.

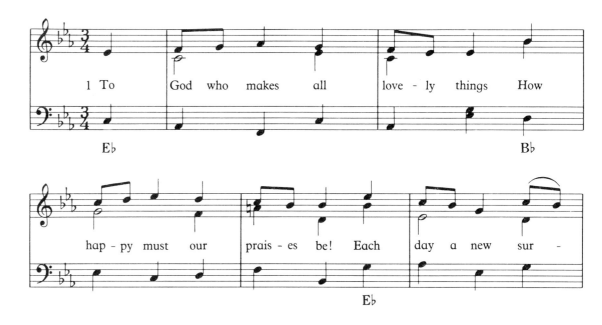

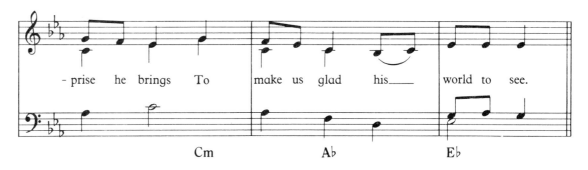

Words: J. M. C. Crum (1872–1958)
Music: Irish traditional melody
Name of tune: Daniel

10 Over the earth is a mat of green

Over the earth is a mat of green,
Over the green is dew,
Over the dew are the arching trees,
Over the trees the blue.
Across the blue are scudding clouds,
Over the clouds, the sun,
Over it all is the love of God,
Blessing us every one,
Blessing us every one.

Words: Ruth Brown
Music: Scots tune, adapted and arranged by Herbert Wiseman (1886–1966)

11 The sun that shines across the sea

The sun that shines across the sea,
The wind that whispers in the tree,
The lark that carols in the sky,
The fleecy clouds a-sailing by—
O, I am rich as rich can be,
For all these things belong to me!
O, I am rich as rich can be,
For all these things are mine,
For all these things are mine!

Words: *Author unknown*
Music: *Dutch folk song*

The descant recorder/glockenspiel part might be used as an alternative accompaniment, or it might be used for a repeat of the hymn while the non-instrumentalists sing, hum or listen.

The children might like to write additional words for the first four lines, incorporating those things or qualities which make them feel "rich".

12 I love the sun

1. I love the sun,
   It shines on me,
   God made the sun,
   And God made me.

2. I love the stars,
   They twinkle on me,
   God made the stars,
   And God made me.

3. I love the rain,
   It splashes on me,
   God made the rain,
   And God made me.

4. I love the wind,
   It blows round me,
   God made the wind,
   And God made me.

5. I love the birds,
   They sing to me,
   God made the birds,
   And God made me.

Some verses might be accompanied by two descant recorders, one playing the part given and the other playing the melody.

Words and music: Gwen F. Smith

13 We praise you for the sun

1. We praise you for the sun,
   The golden, shining sun,
   That gives us healing, strength and joy,
   We praise you for the sun.

2. We praise you for the rain,
   The softly falling rain,
   That gives us healing, strength and joy,
   We praise you for the rain.

3. We praise you for your love,
   Our friend and Father God,
   Who gives us healing, strength and joy,
   We praise you for your love.

The percussion parts suggested for the second, fourth and eighth bars will help the children to keep time on the long sustained notes.

Words: Alice M. Pullen
Music: G. Paisello, based on an old English air
Name of tune: Ceres

14 Stand up, clap hands, shout thank you, Lord

Stand up, clap hands, shout thank you, Lord,
Thank you for the world I'm in.
Stand up, clap hands, shout thank you, Lord,
For happiness and peace within.

1 I look around and the sun's in the sky,
I look around and then I think oh my!
The world is such a wonderful place,
And all because of the Good Lord's grace:

2 I look around and the creatures I see,
I look around and it amazes me
That every fox and bird and hare
Must fit in a special place somewhere:

3 I look around at all the joy I've had,
I look around and then it makes me glad
That I can offer thanks and praise
To him who guides me through my days:

Words: Roger Dyer
Music: Alan Forrest

Hand clapping might be used to accompany the singing of the chorus. The children could quite simply clap on the first and third beats of each bar all the way through, or they might add an extra clap on the fourth and eighth bars, as indicated by the crosses over the music.

15 Think of a world without any flowers

1. Think of a world without any flowers,
   Think of a world without any trees,
   Think of a sky without any sunshine,
   Think of the air without any breeze.
   We thank you, Lord,
      for flowers and trees and sunshine,
   We thank you, Lord,
      and praise your holy name.

2. Think of the world without any animals,
   Think of a field without any herd,
   Think of a stream without any fishes,
   Think of a dawn without any bird.
   We thank you, Lord,
      for all your living creatures,
   We thank you, Lord,
      and praise your holy name.

3. Think of a world without any people,
   Think of a street with no-one living there,
   Think of a town without any houses,
   No-one to love and nobody to care.
   We thank you, Lord,
      for families and friendships,
   We thank you, Lord,
      and praise your holy name.

Words: Doreen Newport. The full text of this hymn, which is abbreviated, may be found in 'New Songs for the Church'
Music: G. C. Westcott
Name of tune: Genesis

16 For all the strength we have

1 For all the strength we have,
   To run and leap and play,
   For all our limbs so sound and strong,
   We thank you, Lord, today.

2 Make all your children, Lord,
   Healthy and strong like me,
   To run and leap and shout and play,
   And praise you in our glee.

Words: Maria M. Penstone
Music: English form of French melody
Name of tune: Zachary

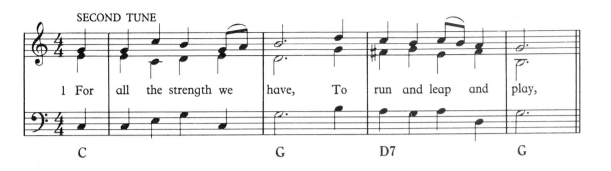
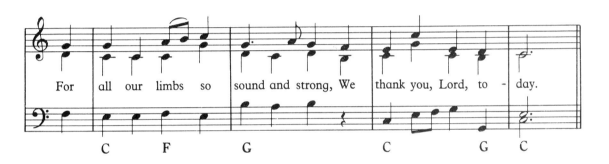

Music: English traditional carol
Name of tune: Sandys

17 Milk bottle tops and paper bags

1. Milk bottle tops and paper bags,
   Iron bedsteads, dirty old rags,
   Litter on the pavement,
   Paper in the park,
   Is this what we
       CLAP CLAP CLAP CLAP
   Really want to see?
       CLAP CLAP CLAP-CLAP CLAP
   No! No! No!

2. Old plastic bottles, silver foil,
   Chocolate wrapping, engine oil,
   Rubbish in the gutter,
   Junk upon the beach,
   Is this what we
       CLAP CLAP CLAP CLAP
   Really want to see?
       CLAP CLAP CLAP-CLAP CLAP
   No! No! No!

3. Help us, Lord, to find each day
   Ways to help to keep away
   That litter off the pavement,
   That rubbish off the beach.
   For this is what we
       CLAP CLAP CLAP CLAP
   Really want to see.
       CLAP CLAP CLAP-CLAP CLAP
   Yes! Yes! Yes!

Words: Peggy Blakeley
Music: Don Harper

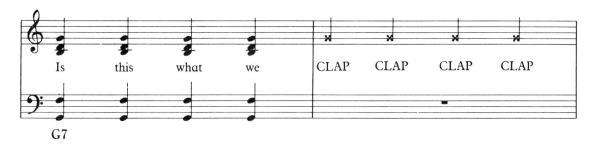
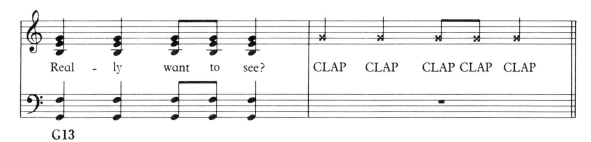
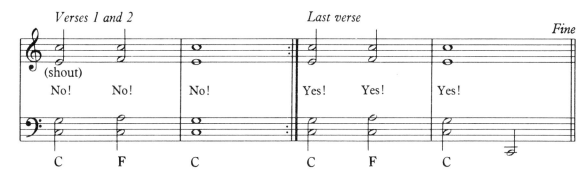

18 Give to us eyes

1. Give to us eyes
   That we may truly see,
   Flight of a bird,
   The shapes in a tree,
   Curve of a hillside,
   Colours in a stone,
   Give to us seeing eyes, O Lord.

2. Give to us ears
   That we may truly hear,
   Music in birdsong,
   Rippling water clear,
   Whine of the winter wind,
   Laughter of a friend,
   Give to us hearing ears, O Lord.

3. Give to us hands
   That we may truly know,
   Patterns in tree bark,
   Crispness of the snow,
   Smooth feel of velvet,
   Shapes in a shell,
   Give to us knowing hands, O Lord.

Words: Peggy Blakeley
Music: Don Harper

19 He gave me eyes so I could see

1. He gave me eyes so I could see
   The wonders of the world.
   Without my eyes I could not see
   The other boys and girls.
   He gave me ears so I could hear
   The wind and rain and sea.
   I've got to tell it to the world,
   He made me.

2. He gave me lips so I could speak
   And say what's in my mind.
   Without my lips I could not speak
   A single word or line.
   He made my mind so I could think,
   And choose what I should be.
   I've got to tell it to the world,
   He made me.

3. He gave me hands so I could touch,
   And hold a thousand things.
   I need my hands to help me write,
   To help me fetch and bring.
   These feet he made so I could run,
   He meant me to be free.
   I've got to tell it to the world,
   He made me.

Words and music: Alan Pinnock
Title: He made me

This arrangement for chime bars and two descant recorders (one playing the melody) is meant to be used without the piano and can be used as an alternative accompaniment to one of the verses. Here it is shown as an accompaniment to the second verse.

Any one of the parts can be used separately with the piano.

20 Praise to God for things we see

1. Praise to God for things we see,
   The growing flower, the waving tree,
   Our mother's face, the bright blue sky
   Where birds and clouds go floating by,
   Praise to God for seeing.

2. Praise to God for things we hear,
   The voices of our playmates dear,
   The merry bells, the song of birds,
   Stories and tunes and kindly words,
   Praise to God for hearing.

Words : Maria M. Penstone
Music : Kenneth G. Finlay

21 Hands to work and feet to run

1. Hands to work and feet to run –
   God's good gifts to me and you;
   Hands and feet he gave to us
   To help each other the whole day through.

2. Eyes to see and ears to hear –
   God's good gifts to me and you;
   Eyes and ears he gave to us
   To help each other the whole day through.

3. Minds to think and hearts to love –
   God's good gifts to me and you;
   Minds and hearts he gave to us
   To help each other the whole day through.

Words: Hilda M. Dodd
Music: G. C. Westcott
Name of tune: Cino Tatnep

22 I'm very glad of God

1. I'm very glad of God:
   His love takes care of me,
   In every lovely thing I see
   God smiles at me!

2. I'm very glad of God:
   His love takes care of me,
   In every lovely sound I hear
   God speaks to me!

The children might enjoy writing extra verses for the senses of smell, touch and taste.

Words and music: Alice M. Pullen

23 Kum ba yah

1. Kum ba yah, my Lord, kum ba yah,
   Kum ba yah, my Lord, kum ba yah,
   Kum ba yah, my Lord, kum ba yah,
   O Lord, kum ba yah.

2. Someone's singing, Lord, kum ba yah

3. Someone's praying, Lord, kum ba yah

4. Someone's hungry, Lord, kum ba yah

5. Someone's suffering, Lord, kum ba yah

6. Someone's lonely, Lord, kum ba yah

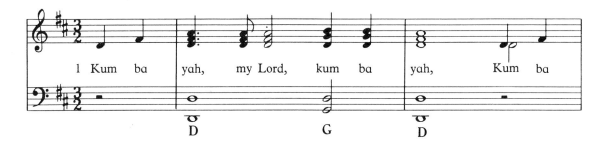
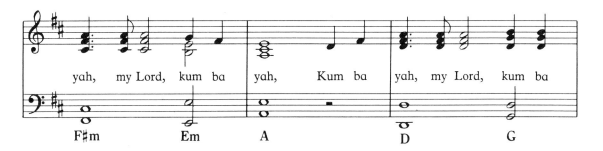
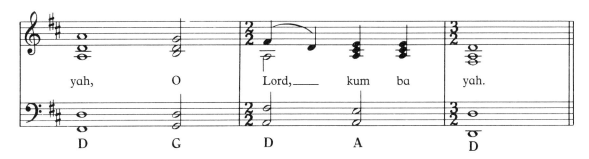

"Kum ba yah" means "come by here" or "be with us".

Words and music: Traditional West Indian
Arranged by Colin Hodgetts

24 A little tiny bird

1. A little tiny bird,
   With sweet and cheerful song,
   God watches, thinks and cares for
   All the day long.

2. A little helpless babe,
   That knows not right from wrong,
   God wakes a mother's love for
   All the day long.

3. A little trustful child,
   Singing to God his song,
   God loves to hear the music
   All the day long.

This hymn might be accompanied by two descant recorders, one playing the part given and the other playing the melody.

Words: H. King Lewis
Music: Hermann von Müller
Name of tune: Froebel

25 Can you count the stars?

1. Can you count the stars that brightly
   Twinkle in the midnight sky?
   Can you count the clouds, so lightly
   O'er the meadows floating by?
   God, the Lord, doth mark their number
   With his eyes that never slumber;
   He hath made them,
   He hath made them,
   He hath made them, every one.

2. Do you know how many children
   Rise each morning bright and gay?
   Can you count their jolly voices,
   Singing sweetly day by day?
   God hears all the happy voices,
   In their merry songs rejoices;
   And he loves them,
   And he loves them,
   And he loves them, every one.

Words: *Johann W. Hey, tr. H. W. Dulcken*
Music: *Melody by J. Lloyd Williams (1855–1928)
   harmonised by M. F. Shaw (1875–1958)*
Name of tune: *Trefaenan*

26 When lamps are lighted in the town

1. When lamps are lighted in the town,
   The boats sail out to sea;
   The fishers watch when night comes down,
   They work for you and me.

2. When little children go to rest,
   Before they sleep, they pray
   That God will bless the fishermen
   And bring them back at day.

3. The boats come in at early dawn,
   When children wake in bed;
   Upon the beach the boats are drawn,
   And all the nets are spread.

4. God has watched o'er the fishermen
   Far on the deep dark sea,
   And brought them safely home again,
   Where they are glad to be.

The part for chime bars uses E and A only and is very simple to play.

Words : Maria M. Penstone
Music : F. H. Barthélémon
Name of tune : Ballerma

27 God bless the grass

1. God bless the grass
   that grows through the crack,
   They roll the concrete over it
   to try and keep it back.
   The concrete gets tired
   of what it has to do,
   It breaks and it buckles
   and the grass grows through;
   And God bless the grass.

2. God bless the truth
   that fights towards the sun,
   They roll the lies over it
   and hope that it is done.
   It moves through the ground
   and reaches for the air,
   And after a while
   it is growing everywhere;
   And God bless the truth.

Words and music : Malvina Reynolds

28 The journey of life

1. The journey of life
   May be easy, may be hard,
   There'll be danger on the way;
   With Christ at my side
   I'll do battle as I ride
   'Gainst the foe that would lead me astray:

   > Will you ride, ride, ride
   > With the King of Kings,
   > Will you follow my leader true;
   > Will you shout Hosanna
   > To the lowly Son of God,
   > Who died for me and you?

2. My burden is light
   And a song is in my heart
   As I travel on life's way;
   For Christ is my Lord
   And he's given me his word
   That by my side he'll stay:

Words and music: V. Collison
Title: Follow my leader

Children will enjoy a percussion accompaniment to the chorus (two pairs of coconut shells, perhaps). The following rhythm is suggested:

29 I danced in the morning

1. I danced in the morning
   When the world was begun,
   And I danced in the moon
   And the stars and the sun,
   And I came down from heaven
   And I danced on the earth –
   At Bethlehem I had my birth.

   Dance, then, wherever you may be,
   I am the Lord of the Dance, said he,
   And I'll lead you all, wherever you may be,
   And I'll lead you all in the dance, said he.

2. I danced for the scribe
   And the pharisee,
   But they would not dance
   And they wouldn't follow me.
   I danced for the fishermen,
   For James and John –
   They came with me
   And the dance went on.

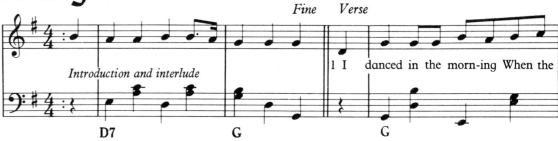
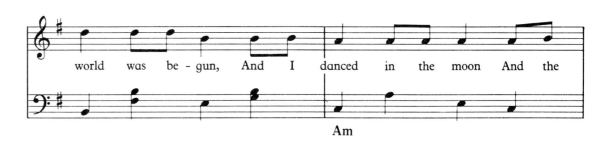

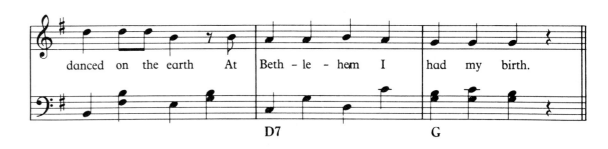

Words and music: Sydney Carter
The full text of this hymn, which is abbreviated, may be found in 'Songs of Sydney Carter. In the Present Tense' Book 2
Title: Lord of the Dance

This tune gives children a wonderful opportunity to explore the rhythm make-up of different bars. Any one of the following rhythms (the bar number is given in each case) could be chosen and repeated throughout by clapping or playing percussion instruments such as triangles or maracas.

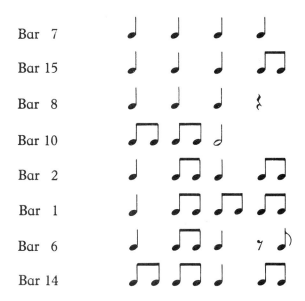

30 Now Jesus one day

1. Now Jesus one day
   Went down to the shore,
   And hundreds of people
   Who'd heard him before
   Followed him to listen,
   Followed him to listen,
   And the waves all went splash,
   splash, splash, splash.

2. He got in a boat
   And put out to sea
   Where people could see him
   As plain as could be.
   They settled down to listen,
   Settled down to listen,
   And the waves all went splash,
   splash, splash, splash.

3. Then he sent them home
   To village and town,
   And he said to Peter:
   "Now, let your net down."
   Peter started fishing,
   Peter started fishing,
   And the waves all went splash,
   splash, splash, splash.

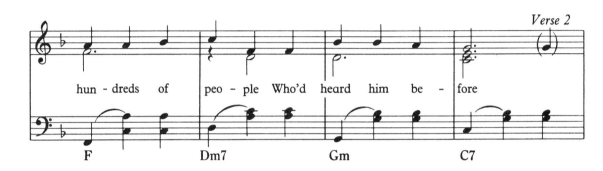

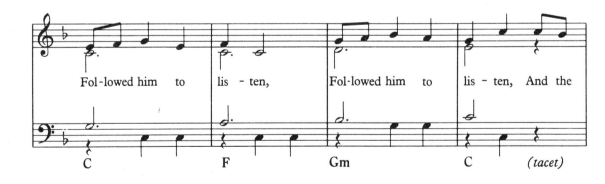

Words and melody: Sister Oswin
Piano accompaniment: Sister Margaret of Sion
Title: Jesus and Peter

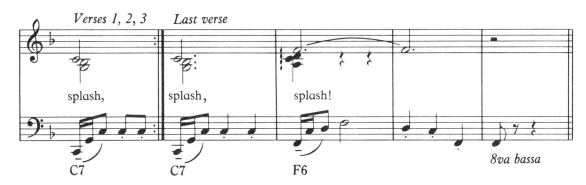

4. The fishes swarmed in;
   The net nearly broke.
   Then Jesus said to him:
   "Come fishing for folk.
   Come and follow me,
   Come and follow me,"
   And the waves all went splash,
   splash, splash, splash,
   splash!

31 It fell upon a summer day

1. It fell upon a summer day,
   When Jesus walked in Galilee,
   The mothers from a village brought
   Their children to his knee.

2. He took them in his arms, and laid
   His hands on each remembered head;
   "Suffer these little ones to come
   To me," he gently said.

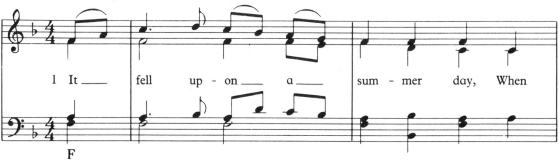
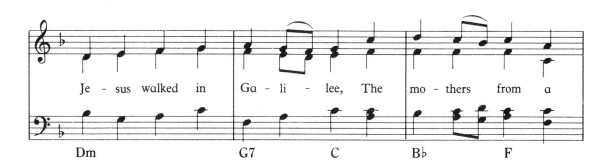
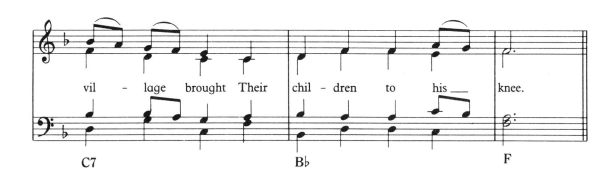

This hymn could be accompanied by two descant recorders, one playing the melody and the other the alto line (the notes in the treble clef with stems pointing downwards). This second part can either be played as written, or an octave higher, giving the effect of a descant to the melody.

Words: Stopford A. Brooke
Music: H. Walford Davies (1869–1941)
Name of tune: Childhood

32 Who's that sitting in the sycamore tree?

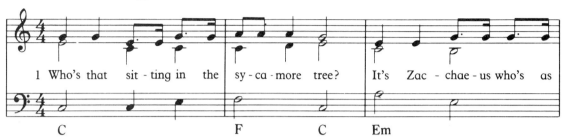

1. Who's that sitting in the sycamore tree?
   It's Zacchaeus who's as mean as can be.
   Down on the ground, he's so short he cannot see
   Over the crowd to Jesus.

   *Come down, Zacchaeus, down from the tree.
   Come down, Zacchaeus, give the Lord his tea.*

2. Who's that coming down the Jericho street?
   Hot and hungry on his two tired feet?
   He's the one whom the crowd has come to greet,
   Raising three cheers for Jesus.

3. Who'll take Jesus home for tea and a rest?
   Each one there would welcome him as a guest.
   Surely he'll pick out the holiest and the best:
   But up in the tree looks Jesus.

4. Who's that knocking at the poor folk's door?
   Sharing his money as he's never done before?
   It's Zacchaeus who's not mean any more;
   All for the love of Jesus.

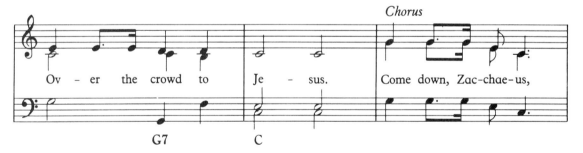

Words and melody: Sister Oswin
Piano accompaniment: G. C. Westcott

33 Jesus' hands were kind hands

1. Jesus' hands were kind hands,
   Doing good to all;
   Healing pain and sickness,
   Blessing children small;
   Washing tired feet
   And saving those who fall;
   Jesus' hands were kind hands,
   Doing good to all.

2. Take my hands, Lord Jesus,
   Let them work for you,
   Make them strong and gentle,
   Kind in all I do;
   Let me watch you, Jesus,
   Till I'm gentle too,
   Till my hands are kind hands,
   Quick to work for you.

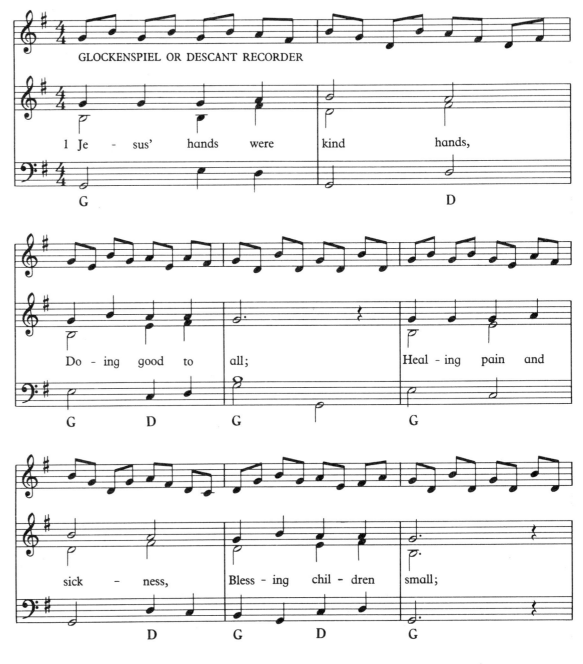

Words: Margaret Cropper
Music: Old French tune
Name of tune: Au clair de la lune

34 When a knight won his spurs

1. When a knight won his spurs,
   In the stories of old,
   He was gentle and brave,
   He was gallant and bold;
   With a shield on his arm
   And a lance in his hand,
   For God and for valour
   He rode through the land.

2. No charger have I
   And no sword by my side,
   Yet still to adventure
   And battle I ride,
   Though back into storyland
   Giants have fled,
   And the knights are no more
   And the dragons are dead.

3. Let faith be my shield
   And let joy be my steed,
   'Gainst the dragons of anger,
   The ogres of greed;
   And let me set free,
   With the sword of my youth,
   From the castle of darkness
   The power of the truth.

Words: Jan Struther (1901–1953)
Music: Melody collected by Cecil J. Sharp, harmonised and arranged by
   R. Vaughan Williams (1872–1958)
Name of tune: Stowey

35 When I needed a neighbour

1. When I needed a neighbour,
    Were you there, were you there?
   When I needed a neighbour,
    Were you there?
      And the creed and the colour
        and the name won't matter,
      Were you there?

2. I was hungry and thirsty

3. I was cold, I was naked

4. When I needed a shelter

5. Wherever you travel,
    I'll be there, I'll be there,
   Wherever you travel,
    I'll be there.
      And the creed and the colour
        and the name won't matter,
      I'll be there.

One suggestion for percussion accompaniment is given but others may be suggested by the children.

Words and music: Sydney Carter
  The full text of this hymn, which is abbreviated, may be found in 'Songs of Sydney Carter. In the Present Tense' Book 3

36 Look out for loneliness

1. Look out for loneliness
   If it should come your way,
   Look out for loneliness,
   Watch for it every day.
   Look at home, look in school,
   When you're shopping with your mum,
   In the classroom, in the playground
   Watch if lonely children come.
       Look out, look out, look out
       For loneliness.

2. Look out for sadness
   Every once in a while,
   Look out for sadness
   And give a friendly smile.
   Give some love,
   Give some warmth
   Give a hand in friendship too;
   Bear in mind that one day soon
   That sad one might quite well be you.
       Look out, look out, look out,
       For loneliness.

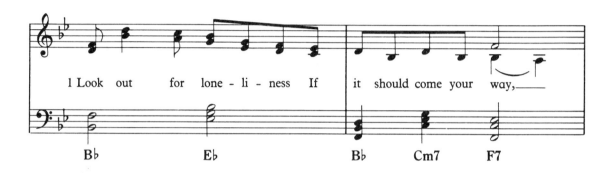
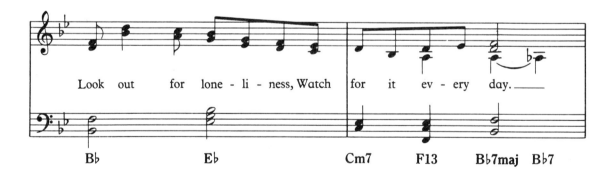

Words : Peggy Blakeley
Music : Don Harper

37 If I had a hammer

1. If I had a hammer,
   I'd hammer in the morning,
   I'd hammer in the evening
   All over this land.
   I'd hammer out danger,
   I'd hammer out a warning,
   I'd hammer out love between
   My brothers and my sisters,
   All over this land.

2. If I had a bell,
   I'd ring it in the morning,
   I'd ring it in the evening
   All over this land.
   I'd ring out danger,
   I'd ring out a warning,
   I'd ring out love between
   My brothers and my sisters,
   All over this land.

3. If I had a song,
   I'd sing it in the morning,
   I'd sing it in the evening
   All over this land.
   I'd sing out danger,
   I'd sing out a warning,
   I'd sing out love between
   My brothers and my sisters,
   All over this land.

Words and music: Lee Hays and Pete Seeger
Piano accompaniment: G. C. Westcott

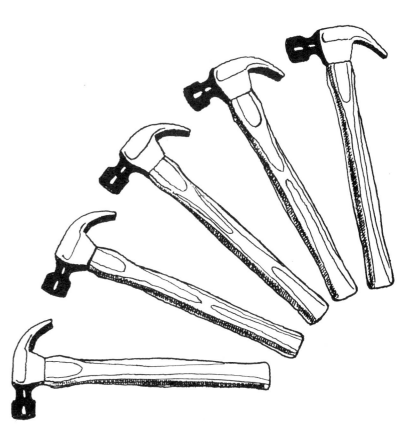

38 Think, think on these things

1. Think, think on these things:
   Being a friend,
   Giving a smile,
   Or helping to make
   Someone else's day worthwhile;
   Think, think on these things.

2. Think, think on these things:
   Unhappy and lost,
   Friendless or old,
   Or what it is like
   To be hungry, to be cold;
   Think, think on these things.

3. Think, think on these things:
   Forgiving an ill,
   Lending a hand,
   Or trying to make
   Other people understand;
   Think, think on these things.

Words: Peggy Blakeley
Music: Don Harper

All three verses can follow the same pattern, finishing at the end of bar 12 in each case, perhaps repeating the words of the last line of the hymn to finish.

The optional coda suggests an alternative ending to the hymn. Here music and words are meant to get softer and softer until they fade away.

39 The ink is black, the page is white

1. The ink is black, the page is white,
   Together we learn to read and write,
   To read and write.
   And now a child can understand,
   This is the law of all the land,
   All the land!
   The ink is black, the page is white,
   Together we learn to read and write,
   To read and write.

2. The board is black, the chalk is white,
   The words stand out so clear and bright,
   So clear and bright.
   And now at last we plainly see
   The alphabet of liberty,
   Liberty!
   The board is black, the chalk is white,
   The words stand out so clear and bright,
   So clear and bright.

3. A child is black, a child is white,
   The whole world looks upon the sight,
   A beautiful sight.
   For very well the whole world knows,
   This is the way that freedom grows,
   Freedom grows!
   A child is black, a child is white,
   The whole world looks upon the sight,
   A beautiful sight.

Words: David Arkin
Music: Earl Robinson

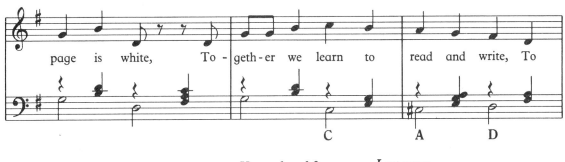

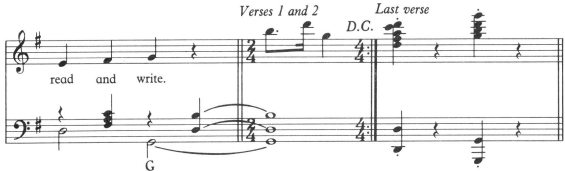

The children might echo the rhythm of the third and sixth lines of the hymn by clapping (as indicated by the crosses over the music).

40 O Jesus, we are well and strong

1. O Jesus, we are well and strong,
   And we can run about and play;
   But there are children who are sick,
   And have to be in bed all day.

2. We thank you for our health and strength;
   And, loving Lord, we pray you, bless
   The children who are weak and ill
   And suffer pain and weariness.

3. Lord, give us thoughtful, loving hearts;
   Show us kind deeds which we may do
   To help some sad or suffering one
   Till they are well and happy too.

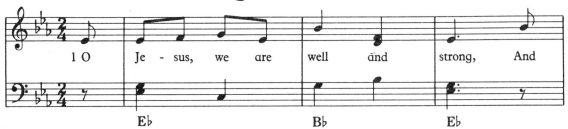
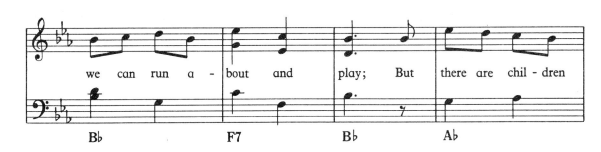

Words: E. F. B. MacAlister (adapted)
Music: Swiss traditional melody
Name of tune: Solothurn

41 All things which live below the sky

1. All things which live below the sky,
   Or move within the sea,
   Are creatures of the Lord most high,
   And brothers unto me.

2. I love to hear the robin sing,
   Perched on the highest bough;
   To see the rook with purple wing
   Follow the shining plough.

3. I love to watch the swallow skim
   The river in his flight;
   To mark, when day is growing dim,
   The glow worm's silvery light.

4. Almighty Father, King of kings,
   The lover of the meek,
   Make me a friend of helpless things,
   Defender of the weak.

Two descant recorders might be used, one playing the melody.

Words: Edward J. Brailsford
Music: Melody collected by R. Vaughan Williams (1872–1958)
Name of tune: Rodmell

42 I love God's tiny creatures

1. I love God's tiny creatures
   That wander wild and free,
   The coral-coated ladybird,
   The velvet humming-bee;
   Shy little flowers in hedge and dyke
   That hide themselves away:
   God paints them, though they are so small,
   God makes them bright and gay.

2. Dear Father, who has all things made,
   And cares about them all,
   There's none too great for your great love,
   Nor anything too small:
   If you can spend such tender care
   On things that grow so wild,
   How wonderful your love must be
   For me, your loving child.

Words: G. W. Briggs (1875–1959)
Music: Roger H. Pope
Name of tune: Southrepps

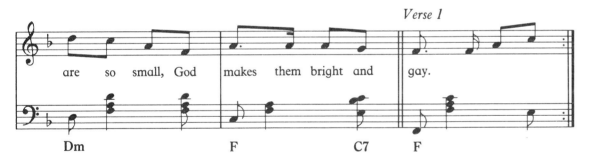

43 Little birds in winter time

1. Little birds in winter time
   Hungry are and poor;
   Feed them, for the Father's sake,
   Till the winter's o'er.

2. Throw them crumbs that you can spare
   Round about your door;
   Feed them, for the Father's sake,
   Till the winter's o'er.

Words: Frederick A. Jackson
Music: 1 Norah C. E. Byrne
2 English traditional melody (St Issey)

44 Who built the ark?

Who built the ark?
Noah, Noah,
Who built the ark?
Brother Noah built the ark.

1. Now in come the animals two by two,
   Hippopotamus and kangaroo.

2. Now in come the animals four by four,
   Two through the window and two
       through the door.

3. Now in come the animals six by six,
   Elephant laughed at the monkey's tricks.

4. Now in come the animals eight by eight,
   Some were on time and the others were late.

5. Now in come the animals ten by ten,
   Five black roosters and five black hens.

6. Now Noah says, go shut that door,
   The rain's started dropping
       and we can't take more.

Words and melody: J. Rosamund Johnson
Piano accompaniment: G. C. Westcott

45   5, 4, 3, 2, 1 and zero

1. 5, 4, 3, 2, 1 and zero,
   Signals blast off into space,
   Men in a rocket ride the sky,
   Boom, boom, boom
   On a journey to the moon.

2. Crackle, squeak through the atmosphere-o
   Voices echo down to earth,
   Men in a module come to rest,
   Boom, boom, boom
   On the highlands of the moon.

3. When they scan the universe-o
   They must see our tiny world,
   Part of a pattern made by God,
   Boom, boom, boom
   From the cold light of the moon.

4. Floating on a parachute-o
   Through to splash-down, back to earth,
   Thank you God, for this world you gave us,

(Either)   Boom, boom, boom,
   So unlike the cold old moon.

(Or)   Quite unlike the stark old moon,
   Quite unlike the cold old moon,
   Quite unlike that old unfriendly moon,
   Boom, boom.

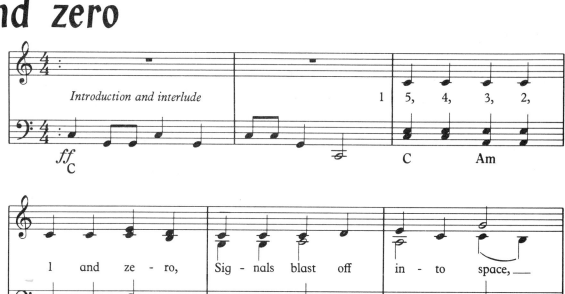

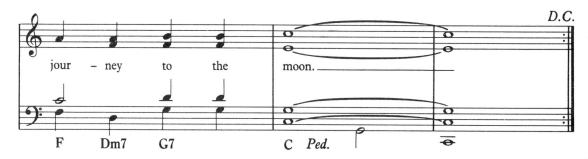

Words: Peggy Blakeley
Music: Don Harper
Title: *A journey to the moon*

The fourth verse of this hymn can be sung quite simply as a five-line verse on the same pattern as the others, using only the music on the opposite page.

If desired, the last verse can be extended to seven lines by including the coda given on this page. In this case the first three lines of the verse will be used with the music as far as the sign ⊕, followed immediately by the last four lines of the verse to the music given on this page.

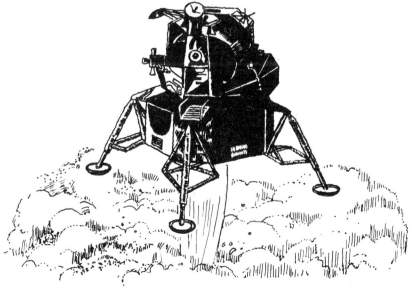

46 Twinkle, twinkle, little star

1. Twinkle, twinkle, little star,
   How I wonder what you are,
   Up above the world so high,
   Like a diamond in the sky.

   Twinkle, twinkle, little star,
   How I wonder what you are.

2. When the blazing sun is gone,
   When he nothing shines upon,
   Then you show your little light,
   Twinkle, twinkle all the night.

3. Then the traveller in the dark
   Thanks you for your tiny spark;
   Could he see which way to go
   If you did not twinkle so?

Words: Jane Taylor
Music: G. C. Westcott
Name of tune: Glyn

One descant recorder might play the melody of this second tune and a second descant recorder the alto part (the notes in the treble clef with tails pointing downwards).

Music to second tune : Joseph Smith
Name of tune : Innocents

47 God who put the stars in space

1. God who put the stars in space,
   Who made the world we share,
   In his making made a place
   For me, and put me here.

2. Thank you, God, for stars in space
   And for the world we share.
   Thank you for my special place
   To love and serve you here.

The four bars of introduction and the last line of the piano accompaniment are entirely optional.

Words: L. S. Reed
Music: G. C. Westcott
Name of tune: Harpers

48 All the flowers are waking

1. All the flowers are waking,
   Spring has come again;
   God has sent the sunshine,
   God has sent the rain.

2. All the trees are waking,
   Spring has come again;
   God has sent the sunshine,
   God has sent the rain.

3. All the birds are singing,
   Spring has come again;
   Singing in the sunshine,
   Singing in the rain.

   A verse for Winter

4. All the flowers are sleeping
   Underneath the ground;
   Sleeping in the winter,
   Sleeping safe and sound.

Words: adapted by Winifred E. Barnard
Music: Eric G. Barnard

49 In the early morning

1. In the early morning,
   Listen to the lark
   Singing in the daylight,
   Singing out the dark.
   In the early springtime
   Hear the thrushes sing,
   Singing out the winter,
   Singing in the spring.

2. Where the dead leaves rustle
   Under winter trees,
   Everywhere are rising
   Wood anemones;
   Where the snow was lying
   Dead and white and chill,
   Celandines and daisies
   Cover all the hill.

3. Jesus loved the lilies,
   Jesus loved the birds –
   They'd be singing with us
   If they knew the words!
   O, let us say clearly
   What they try to say,
   Birds and buds and children
   Thanking him today.

Words: J. M. C. Crum (1872–1958)
Music: adapted and arranged by M. F. Shaw (1875–1958)
Name of tune: Gamble

50 Hurray for Jesus

Hurray for Jesus,
Riding to Jerusalem,
Riding to the city
Up a steep and dusty track.
Hurray for Jesus,
Riding to Jerusalem,
Riding there in triumph
On a little donkey's back.

1. Wave palms in the air,
   Spread your bright cloaks everywhere
   And sing, sing, sing.
   Shout out: This is great.
   Jesus enters through the gate –
   Our King.

2. Children wild with joy –
   Every girl and every boy;
   They wave, wave, wave.
   Only we know why
   Christ our King has come to die,
   And save.

Words and melody: Sister Oswin
Piano accompaniment: Sister Margaret of Sion
Title: A Welcome Song

51 We have a king who rides a donkey

1. We have a king who rides a donkey,
   We have a king who rides a donkey,
   We have a king who rides a donkey
   And his name is Jesus.

   Jesus, the king, is risen,
   Jesus, the king, is risen,
   Jesus, the king, is risen
   Early in the morning.

2. Trees are waving a royal welcome (3 times)
   For the king called Jesus.

3. We have a king who cares for people (3 times)
   And his name is Jesus.

4. What shall we do with our life this morning? (3 times)
   Give it up in service!

Words: Fred Kaan. The full text of this hymn, which is abbreviated, may be found in 'Pilgrim Praise'
Music: What shall we do with a drunken sailor?

Two piano and guitar arrangements of this tune are given so that accompanists can choose which they prefer, or play a different accompaniment to different verses.

Accompaniment to alternative version: G. C. Westcott

52 Who can see the great wind blow?

1. Who can see the great wind blow?
   Neither I nor you.
   But it blows the clouds along,
   Blows the grass and branches strong.
   I can feel the great wind blow,
   So can all of you.

2. Who can see God's spirit come?
   Neither I nor you.
   But he helps us to be strong,
   Loving good and fighting wrong.
   I can feel God's spirit come,
   So can all of you.

Words: Margaret Cropper
Music: A. R. B. Wylam
Name of tune: Halvergate

53 The flowers that grow in the garden

1. The flowers that grow in the garden
   Dance in the sun,
   Dance in the sun,
   The flowers that grow in the garden
   Thank the Lord for the sun.

2. The birds that fly in the tree tops

3. The cows and sheep in the meadows

4. The fish that swim in the river

5. Then let all children gaily singing

The part for individual chime bars, using only D and G, is very suitable for younger children. This does not, however, fit in with the harmonies of the piano accompaniment, so when chime bars are used it is suggested that descant recorders play the melody and the piano is silent.

Chime bars and recorder accompaniment could alternate with piano accompaniment.

Words : Barbara Hagon
Music : Swedish melody

54 Look for signs that summer's done

1. Look for signs that summer's done,
   Winter's drawing near.
   Watch the changing colours come,
   Turning of the year.
   See the flowers' final blaze
   In the morning's misty haze,
   Sing a thankful song of praise,
   Autumn time is here.

2. See the fields are bare and brown,
   Feel the nights turn cold.
   Lamps are early lit in town,
   Hunter's moon shines gold.
   Thank you, God, for rest and food,
   For the Harvest safely stored,
   Sing a song to praise the Lord
   As the year grows old.

Words: Peggy Blakeley
Music: Don Harper

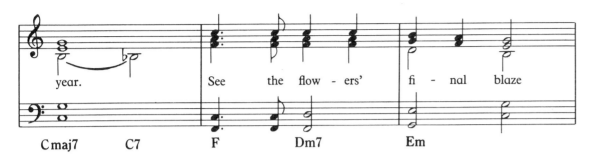

55 When the corn is planted

1. When the corn is planted
   In the deep dark bed,
   Mothers know their children
   Will have daily bread.

2. God sends sun and showers,
   Birds sing overhead,
   While the corn is growing
   For our daily bread.

3. When the corn is gathered,
   Stored in barn and shed,
   Then we all are thankful
   For our daily bread.

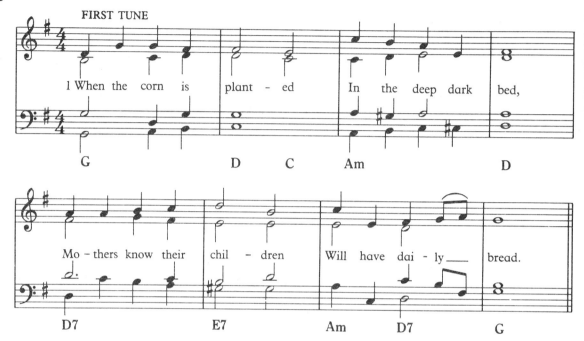

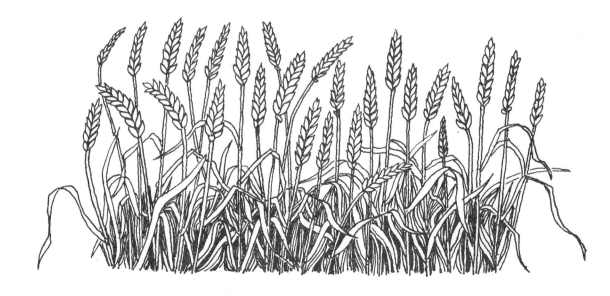

Words: Author unknown
Music: A. H. Mann
Name of tune: Worship

The arrangement below for chime bars and two descant recorders (one playing the melody) is meant to be played without the piano and can be used as an alternative accompaniment to one of the verses.

Music of second tune: T. R. Matthews
Name of tune: North Coates

56 The farmer comes to scatter the seed

1. The farmer comes to scatter the seed,
   Scatter the seed, scatter the seed,
   The farmer comes to scatter the seed
   Over the fields so brown.

2. God sends the sun, God sends the rain,
   Over again, over again,
   God sends the sun, God sends the rain,
   Over the fields so brown.

3. Up come the green shoots peeping through,
   First one by one, then two by two,
   Up come the green shoots peeping through,
   Under the sky so blue.

4. The waving corn all golden brown,
   Golden brown, golden brown,
   The farmer comes to cut it down,
   Under the sky so blue.

5. Then praise our God who makes it grow,
   Makes it grow, makes it grow,
   To feed his people here below,
   Blessing and love to show.

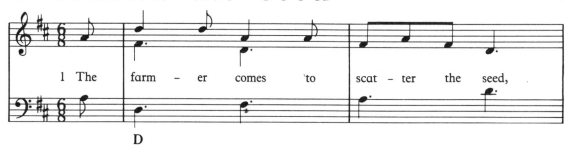
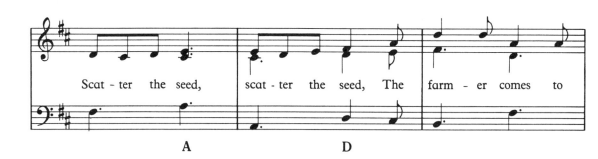

Words: C. Hardie
Music: Traditional (adapted)
Name of tune: Anthony Roly

57 See how the snowflakes are falling

1. See how the snowflakes are falling,
   Falling so gentle and white,
   Coming from God in their beauty,
   All through the day and the night.

2. White are the hills and the meadows,
   White are the roofs of the town,
   Softly, so softly are falling
   Feathery snowflakes down.

The percussion accompaniment suggested uses two triangles maintaining a steady 6/8 rhythm throughout, while individual chime bars, E flat, B flat and A flat, are used to echo the bass note on the first beat of each bar.

Words: Frederick A. Jackson
Music: freely adapted from a German carol melody

58 At half past three we go home to tea

1. At half past three we go home to tea,
   Or maybe at quarter to four;
   And ten pairs of feet go running up the street
   And in at their own front door:
   And it's rough and tumble, rattle and noise,
   Mothers and fathers, girls and boys;
   Baby in the carry-cot, cat by the stove;
   A little bit of quarrelling,
   A lot of love.

2. Lord Jesus taught that his children ought
   To forgive one another each day,
   And to give and take for his dear sake;
   So help us, Lord, we pray:
   For it's rough and tumble, rattle and noise,
   Mothers and fathers, girls and boys;
   Baby in the carry-cot, cat by the stove;
   A little bit of quarrelling,
   But much more love.

Words: Margaret Rose
Music: M. R. Cook

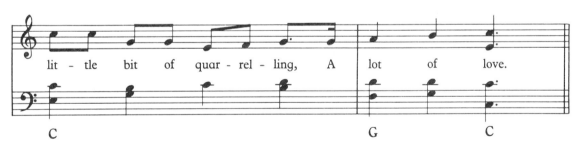

59 We're going home

We're going home, sh, sh,
We're going home, sh, sh,
We're going home to Dad and Mum, sh, sh.
It's time to go, sh, sh,
It's time to go, sh, sh,
Because the day is nearly done, sh, sh.
And now we ask you, God,
Keep us this night
Quite safe from harm
'Till morning light.
We're going home, sh, sh,
We're going home, sh, sh,
And so good night to everyone.

Words: Peggy Blakeley
Music: Don Harper

It is suggested that this hymn might be sung twice, the second time very quietly.

A second part is suggested for descant recorder or glockenspiel. Either of these may be used with piano accompaniment, or the accompaniment may be provided by two recorders, one playing the melody and one the second part.

Index of first lines

A little tiny bird, 24
All the flowers are waking, 48
All things which live below the sky, 41
At half past three we go home to tea, 58

Can you count the stars that brightly? 25
Come, let us remember the joys of the town, 7

Father, we thank you for the night, 1
5, 4, 3, 2, 1 and zero, 45
For all the strength we have, 16

Give to us eyes, 18
God bless the grass that grows through the crack, 27
God who put the stars in space, 47

Hands to work and feet to run, 21
He gave me eyes so I could see, 19
Hurray for Jesus, 50

I danced in the morning, 29
I have seen the golden sunshine, 6
I love God's tiny creatures, 42
I love the sun, 12
If I had a hammer, 37
I'm very glad of God, 22
In the early morning, 49
It fell upon a summer day, 31

Jesus' hands were kind hands, 33

Kum ba yah, my Lord, kum ba yah, 23

Little birds in winter time, 43
Look for signs that summer's done, 54
Look out for loneliness, 36

Lord, I love to stamp and shout, 5

Milk bottle tops and paper bags, 17
Morning has broken, 3

Now Jesus one day, 30

O Jesus, we are well and strong, 40
O Lord! Shout for joy, 4
Over the earth is a mat of green, 10

Praise to God for things we see, 20

See how the snowflakes are falling, 57
Stand up, clap hands, shout thank you, Lord, 14

The farmer comes to scatter the seed, 56
The flowers that grow in the garden, 53
The golden cockerel, 2
The ink is black, the page is white, 39
The journey of life, 28
The sun that shines across the sea, 11
Think of a world without any flowers, 15
Think, think on these things, 38
This is a lovely world, 8
To God who makes all lovely things, 9
Twinkle, twinkle, little star, 46

We have a king who rides a donkey, 51
We praise you for the sun, 13
We're going home, sh, sh, 59
When a knight won his spurs, 34
When I needed a neighbour, 35
When lamps are lighted in the town, 26
When the corn is planted, 55
Who built the ark? 44
Who can see the great wind blow? 52
Who's that sitting in the sycamore tree? 32